John Lennon

by Michael White

BLACKBIRCH™
PRESS

THOMSON

GALE

San Diego • Detroit • New York • San Francisco • Cleveland
New Haven, Conn. • Waterville, Maine • London • Munich

Photo Credits: Hulton Archive/Getty Images: cover; AKG: 40 (top); Camera Press: 10; Gamma: 54; Hulton Deutsch Collection: 12 (top), 27, 43, 46, 47; Kobal Collection: 37 (top), 48 (bottom); London Features International: 13 (top), 30, 44 (left), 51 (bottom), 52; Pictorial Press: 4, 5, 8, 13 (bottom), 15, 16, 18, 21, 22, 23, 24, 25, 26, 29, 31, 33, 34-35, 36, 37 (bottom), 40-41, 44 (top), 45, 48 (top), 50 (top), 53, 55, 57, 58, 59, 60; Popperfoto: 7, 9, 44 (right), 50 (bottom); Rex Features: 54 (top)

LIBRARY OF CONGRESS CATALOGING-IN-PUBLICATION DATA

White, Michael, 1959-
  John Lennon / by Michael White.
      p. cm. — (World musicmakers series)
Includes index.
Summary: Reviews the life and work of legendary rock musician John Lennon, from his childhood in Liverpool to superstardom as a member of the Beatles and as a solo artist, as well as his promotion of world peace.
  ISBN 1-56711-973-5 (hardback : alk. paper)
  1. Lennon, John, 1940-1980—Juvenile literature. 2. Rock musicians—England—Biography—Juvenile literature. [1. Lennon, John, 1940-1980. 2. Musicians. 3. Rock music.] I. Title. II. Series.
  ML3930.L34W45 2004
  782.42166'092—dc21   2003005118

Contents

Pop superstars

It is February 7, 1964, and all day New York radio stations have been playing only Beatles' records. The roads to Kennedy Airport in New York are blocked solid with cars, which have caused a traffic jam that goes halfway back to Manhattan. Every five minutes, local disc jockeys interrupt the music to announce the latest progress of Pan Am flight 101 as it crosses the Atlantic Ocean from London.

On board the plane are four young men. They are national heroes in Great Britain, and the most famous musical group in the history of pop music: John Lennon, Paul McCartney, Ringo Starr, and George Harrison—the Beatles.

A few hours later, the plane lands and the Beatles are escorted out of the airport to a group of waiting limousines. Across the street, ten thousand screaming and hysterical fans throng behind barriers and a cordon of police. As the Beatles appear, the anxious fans crash through the barriers and past the severely outnumbered police and start to run across the street to the cars. The limousines speed off and are followed by a convoy of fans who form a motorcade of hundreds of vehicles all the way to the Plaza Hotel in New York City.

Beatlemania had preceded the group to the United States, one of the most difficult music markets to break into. As the Beatles arrived, their fifth single, "I Want To Hold Your Hand," hit number one on the Billboard Chart. Two days later, they performed on the Ed Sullivan Show, one of the most popular programs on American television. An estimated 73 million people

Opposite: In 1964, John Lennon and fellow Beatles were interviewed upon their arrival in Manhattan for their first American tour.

Below: John Lennon (left) and Paul McCartney (right) wrote most of the group's songs.

saw the interview. Within two months of that appearance, in April 1964, the Beatles would occupy all top five positions in the Billboard Chart at the same time, a feat that has never been—and probably never will be—repeated. There could be no doubt that America had fallen under the "Beatlemania" spell.

Idols

At the time of their first trip to the United States, the Beatles had already become the most famous and successful pop group in Great Britain. They were beloved by huge numbers of frenzied teenage fans who huddled around stage doors, desperate to catch a sight of or even touch, one of their idols. There had never before, in the history of music, been an entertainment phenomenon to match the Beatles, and no single artist or group has come close to matching them since.

In November 1963, the Beatles were invited to perform at the famous annual Royal Variety Show. It was the perfect end to a magical year for the four members of the group from Liverpool, a year in which the British nation had suddenly discovered the music, wit, and charm of the latest music business find. It was in 1963 that the Beatles had their first hit records and were adopted as the darlings of the youth counterculture revolution, as they swept away all the old traditions and limitations of the music scene. By the end of the year, the four "lovable mop-tops" or "Fab Four," as they were affectionately dubbed by the press, were ready to take on the world.

Over the next three decades, as the Beatles and as solo artists, John, Paul, George, and Ringo would among them sell more than 560 million records throughout the world. They would have the most number-one singles and albums of any act of the 1960s: seventeen number-one singles, ten number-one albums and a total of more than one thousand weeks on the music charts of the world.

When the Royal Variety Show was televised, the success of the Beatles soared still further. The single released after the show, "I Want To Hold Your Hand," achieved staggering advance orders of more than one million.

"That the Beatles' 'I Want to Hold Your Hand' was the first single by an English group to rise to the Number One place in the U.S. charts is some sort of tribute to the Beatles' genius in devising an original style and presentation which were appealing not only to the north of England and the entire United Kingdom, but to America and the rest of the world."

—Sandra Shevey, from *The Other Side of Lennon*

John Lennon, leader of the Beatles, was no average pop star, however. Not only did he reach the hearts of millions through his music, but within a few years of the 1963 Royal Variety Show, he would move beyond the world of entertainment to become a powerful campaigner for world peace.

War baby

John Winston Lennon was a "war baby," born during World War II on October 9, 1940, in Liverpool, England. His parents, Julia and Alfred Lennon, had been married for nearly two years when John was born. The couple had seen little of each other in that time because Alfred Lennon was a ship's steward and was often away at sea. He was not at home when John was born and did not see his son until a brief visit to Liverpool many months later.

John Lennon was born in Liverpool, England, (pictured) during World War II.

A week after he was born, John was taken home. Before her son had reached his first birthday, however, Julia Lennon realized that her on-and-off marriage was all but over. She knew that it would present huge problems to raise a small child on her own in war-torn Great Britain, so she decided to accept her sister Mimi's offer to look after the baby.

Mimi was happily married to George Smith, who ran a dairy farm near their home at 251 Menlove Avenue in the comfortable Woolton district of Liverpool. They had no children and adored baby John. Mimi had cared for mother and son ever since Julia had returned from the hospital. She had visited Julia almost every day and helped her to get through the first six months of John's life without the help and support of the baby's father. It was of little surprise, therefore, that Julia Lennon turned to her sister to foster the boy when the pressures of single parenthood grew too great.

John became very attached to his foster parents and he adored his uncle almost as much as his aunt. Julia visited every day, and the bond between mother and son was never broken. George provided the much-needed paternal figure otherwise missing in John's childhood. There is, however, little doubt that John Lennon's strange family background did much to produce many facets of his complex character. As he grew older, there were many influences on his personality, but much of his unusual attitude about life stemmed from these early upheavals. In the years ahead, there would be many more personal problems and challenges. Each of these played its part in shaping John's personality in the same way his childhood experiences did.

A troubled childhood

Before John's second birthday, his mother, Julia, began living with a man named John Dykins. Around the same time, John's father, Alfred, or Freddy, returned home unannounced. Freddy tried desperately to patch up his failed marriage and reunite the family. Julia resisted all such attempts, and Freddy returned to sea again, resentful and bitter. John was left sad and shaken by these events.

In 1946, shortly before John's sixth birthday, Freddy again appeared in Liverpool and made one last attempt to claim his son. Without telling Julia, Freddy took John on a day-trip to the seaside resort of Blackpool.

When Julia discovered what had happened, she was furious. When Freddy did not bring John back to Menlove Avenue that evening, she flew into a panic and set off to find Freddy and to get her son back.

Choice

Julia finally caught up with them at the place where Freddy was staying. After a violent argument between Julia and Freddy, five-year-old John was asked to choose whether he wanted to return with Julia to Liverpool or stay with his father.

Both asked the impossible as they pressured the small boy for an answer to such a terrible question. Confused and frightened as he looked from one angry face to another, John declared that he wanted to stay with his father.

Below: John Lennon's father, Alfred "Freddy" Lennon, was a ship's steward who spent most of his son's childhood at sea.

Triumphant, Freddy suggested that Julia leave. As Julia slammed the door behind her, John changed his mind. As the tears started, he yelled after his mother and ran to the door, flinging himself into her arms. Within hours, John and Julia were back in the oasis of calm at 251 Menlove Avenue, drinking tea in Aunt Mimi's kitchen.

Dovedale

The previous year, John had been enrolled at Dovedale Primary School in Liverpool. Mimi had taken a great deal of trouble to find the best school in the area and had picked Dovedale even though it involved a short bus ride from their house.

John did well at school and his teachers all had a high regard for his academic ability. His only weak subject was mathematics, but he excelled in art. Many marked him as an unusual character, though. He had a large group of friends, of which he was the undoubted leader. Together they avoided the usual games played by most of the other boys. John got involved in numerous fights and would often return home with cuts and scrapes. Although he was not seen as a ruffian by the teachers, there were a number of parents who were wary of him and thought he was a bad influence on their children.

Artist

It soon became clear that John had considerable talent as an artist. When he was ten, he entered one of his pictures in a school exhibition. The picture was a strange drawing of Jesus Christ that was daring enough to raise a few eyebrows among the parents and staff who attended the show.

He did well in the school exams and passed the 11-plus, an exam that used to be taken by all pupils in Great Britain at the age of eleven to determine which type of school they would attend the next year. It was not an easy exam, and very few pupils passed. Those who did went on to attend a grammar school where they were usually expected to achieve a higher academic standard.

Early rebellion

For the remainder of John's time at Dovedale School, Aunt Mimi had little to worry about in regard to his attitude and progress. He became quiet and solitary, and he preferred to spend his summer vacation making solo cycling trips to the countryside. Then, in September 1952, he made the move to Quarry Bank High School, a highly regarded grammar school just a short bicycle ride from his home. Within a few months, everything changed. From day one, his attitude to education, and with it, his success at school, nose-dived.

At Dovedale, he had been top of his class, combining self-assurance with academic success. He immediately decided that at senior school, with its strict uniform code, masters in their academic gowns, and much older boys, the only way he could survive would be to confront the system head-on. From this time on, the rebel in John Lennon began to surface.

His work began to suffer and he slipped down the streams into which the pupils were grouped. He started to cut class and challenged the rules by refusing to wear his uniform in the correct fashion. He also insulted teachers, chased around the corridors, swore, and smoked in the toilets. John never took an interest in school activities, such as sports or clubs, and did his best to disrupt such events whenever possible.

Before long, the smart and friendly primary-school boy had completely changed. By the end of his first term at Quarry Bank School, he had been labeled by the teachers as a troublesome, difficult child who would go nowhere in life. Once stamped with this profile, there was little he could have done about it. John realized this, and rather than try to improve himself, he decided that the only course of action was to carry on the way he had started.

Much to Aunt Mimi's disappointment and in spite of her constant reprimands, John's mind was now set on open confrontation with authority. To those around him, it seemed like there would be little hope for the scruffy, foul-mouthed, tough kid who was rude to

Above: John Lennon (pictured at age nine) attended Dovedale Primary School where he developed a reputation as a bad influence on some of the other children.

Opposite above: Lennon (pictured here at age ten in front of his aunt Mimi's house) chose to remain with his aunt rather than live with his father.

Opposite below: John designed this Christmas card for his aunt Mimi and uncle George.

everyone. He would almost certainly make nothing of his life and would find himself in a dead-end job or, worse, in prison.

An odd fascination

At this time, another disturbing aspect of John's personality started to appear. He began to demonstrate an odd fascination with crippled and disabled people. He spent much of his time drawing haunting images of deformed people and seemed to be obsessed with disease and infirmity. Even his most innocent drawings had an eerie edge to them. The same fascination started to appear in the poetry and rhymes he had recently begun to write, and his sharp wit, so famous in later years, grew increasingly black.

The first of a series of disasters struck John in June 1955, a few months before his fifteenth birthday. Uncle George who, along with Aunt Mimi, had nurtured John into his teens died suddenly. There is little doubt that John was seriously disturbed by his uncle's death, and it played a part in hardening John's attitude to the world.

Rock and roll

In 1955, the world outside Quarry Bank School had begun to change fast. During his final years there, popular culture altered almost overnight, and John was fully aware of the new scene growing around him.

The year 1955 saw the release of a hugely influential film, *Rebel Without a Cause*, which starred a great new talent and teen idol, James Dean. In Dean, the young people of the Western world were exposed to a new kind of hero. Before him, role models—actors such as Cary Grant and Clark Gable and singers like Jimmy Young—had all been much older than their fans. James Dean was the first truly subversive hero, a role model for rebellion, a character who encouraged opposition to the bland morality of parents and grandparents.

At the same time, the world of music was changing with the emergence of a new form of music that had crossed the Atlantic from America. The new music was called rock and roll. It had a lively, up-tempo sound with pounding drums, loud electric guitars, and passionate vocals that spoke openly of youthful desires. Its roots lay in the jazz and blues music that originated in the southern states, but it was a sound stripped bare and very basic. That was where its appeal lay, because it was immediate. Rock and roll music consisted of a simple rhythm played on drums and bass guitar with an aggressive catchy lead guitar part over the top and a strong vocal.

Elvis

Most people over twenty-five hated rock and roll—parents, conservative community leaders, and politicians saw it as a threat to the moral welfare of young people. The youth of the Western world, on the other hand, loved it. John Lennon decided where his future lay. In rock and roll, he immediately saw a way out of his humdrum existence. From the time rock and roll arrived in Great Britain, Lennon became aware that there were others who viewed the world in the same way as he did and who also felt that there was more to life than school and jobs in offices or factories.

Then, one night, early in 1956, John heard a sound that he would never forget, a sound that would eventually propel him into his own musical career. While he was tuned in to Radio Luxembourg, broadcast from the heart of Europe, he heard the opening bars of a song called "Heartbreak Hotel" by an American singer named Elvis Presley. After that, everything changed.

Aunt Mimi did not approve of Elvis Presley. When John begged her to buy him a guitar, she flatly refused. Thwarted, John sent off for one he had seen advertised in a newspaper. Within weeks after he first heard "Heartbreak Hotel" and received the guitar through the mail, John had formed his first music group with friends from school. John was the leader of the band and sang lead vocals. He also organized rehearsals and chose the songs the band would play.

The group was called the Quarry Men, and it played what was known as skiffle, a raw blend of folk, jazz, and rock and roll with an infectious beat and easily

Opposite above: John Lennon grew up listening to jukebox rock and roll of the 1950s and early 1960s.

Above top: Elvis Presley's song "Heartbreak Hotel" inspired young John Lennon.

Above below: James Dean became a role model for rebellious teens in the 1950s.

imitated simplicity. The group rehearsed during lunch breaks at school and after classes at Julia Lennon's house.

By the summer of 1957, the group was ready to play its first "concert." It was at one such performance, a few weeks before he left Quarry Bank School, that John Lennon made an important acquaintance. On July 6, 1957, the Quarry Men played at a church social in Liverpool. They looked completely out of place among the middle-aged women in flowery dresses, and the elderly gentlemen and children who sold cakes from stalls in the summer sunshine. There was sixteen-year-old John Lennon on the makeshift stage with his greased-back hairstyle and tight black jeans, bashing out Elvis Presley hits and "Be-Bop-a-Lula" at top volume. It is hardly surprising that the local residents and church helpers working at the gathering that day were not terribly impressed.

There was at least one person in the audience who was very interested in the sound he heard, however. He was a tall, well-built fifteen-year-old with a round, handsome face and longish brown hair. He watched the whole performance and applauded enthusiastically after each song. His name was Paul McCartney.

The beginning

1957 was an important year for John Lennon. In September, he entered the Liverpool College of Art, and in the same month, he began to write songs with Paul McCartney.

The two boys could not have been more different in character. Paul was very conventional and attended the prestigious Liverpool Institute. His father, Jim, was a jazz pianist and had once been a musician. Paul's mother had died in 1956, and with the help of two kindly sisters who lived nearby, Jim had looked after Paul and his brother, Michael. Music was in Paul McCartney's blood, and the family home was a shrine to jazz music. He had learned to play the piano from an early age and was skilled on the guitar as well by the time he met John Lennon.

> "I had a group. I was the singer and the leader. I met Paul and I made the decision whether to have him in or not—was it better to make the group stronger or let me be stronger?—and that decision was to let Paul in. Instead of going for an individual thing we went for the strongest format and for equals."
>
> —John Lennon

As much as they were different in background, John and Paul had one very important interest in common. They were both devoted to rock and roll and had an instant kinship on a musical level. This bound them together through the whirlwind years that would follow. They both realized that Paul was the superior musician, but John had the more rebellious character, the cool rock-and-roll attitude and the youthful aggression that Paul lacked.

John Lennon (at right microphone) and Paul McCartney (at left) were part of a rock-and-roll band called the Quarry Men in 1957.

John, Paul . . .

Within weeks of their first encounter at the church social, Paul and John began to meet up at Paul's house and started to write songs together. Jim McCartney did not approve of his son's new friend and criticized the shady-looking youth's scruffy appearance when he came to the house. To avoid conflict, John and Paul would wait for Paul's father to go to work before John would sneak over and they would get out their guitars and work on their compositions. John and Paul would

. . . .

"John Lennon was every-thing . . . bold, dynamic, free of his parents and family ties. Independent."

—Raymond Feather, who lived near John as a child

. . . .

face each other with their acoustic, or non-electric, guitars and let ideas flow from one to the other. Neither one felt that the other was a better songwriter, they simply bounced tunes and lyrics off each other. The element of competition between them always made them work harder and better. Although the main composer usually sang the song, the pair made a conscious decision to use the joint credit to give them a stronger identity: Lennon and McCartney—a partnership the world will never forget.

Freedom

Liverpool College of Art gave John far more freedom than he had experienced at Quarry Bank. Compared to his old school, it was a very liberal institution. Students were allowed to wear what they liked and there was a more relaxed relationship between students and staff. Despite this, John still managed to gain a reputation as a rebel. He only rarely handed in work and found even the most easygoing members of the staff too strict.

"Ye Cracke" was a bar where John Lennon often socialized during his art school days.

He was very popular with female students and made one very close male friend, Stuart Sutcliffe, who was a talented and dedicated art student. John and Stuart were as close as any two friends could be and spent most of their free time together.

Within his first year at art college, two other important people entered John's life. The first was Cynthia Powell, a strikingly pretty girl who was a fellow student at the college. John and Cynthia immediately struck up an intense relationship.

John, Paul, George . . .

Then, early in 1958, John met George Harrison, a friend of Paul's from the Liverpool Institute. He was three years younger than John, but a fine guitarist. Paul introduced the two of them when he brought George along to one of their daily lunchtime rehearsal sessions that now took place in a free room at the art college.

George was in awe of John Lennon, and it was some time before he was accepted by the older boy. John, however, was quick to realize Harrison's technical ability on the guitar, and by February 1958, George had joined the Quarry Men. The group now consisted of John, Paul, and George at its core, with a collection of friends who came and went as temporary members of the band.

John's musical ambitions had expanded, his new group was set to play live, and he had several close friends and a steady girlfriend. Life in 1958 looked promising for John Lennon. If the college authorities did not see him as a hopeful student, he felt confident that, given time, things would work out for him in music.

Tragedy

Then, another tragedy struck. In July 1958, John's mother, Julia Lennon, was run down and killed by a car. John reacted to the death of his mother as he had done when his uncle George had died only three years earlier. He closed in upon himself and spoke about it to no one. He felt as though he had lost his mother twice: once when he was sent to live with his aunt and

• •

"[John] was rough and ready and not my type at all, to start off with, but again, this enigmatic character you couldn't resist. . . . He walked around without his glasses, a guitar over his shoulder and a look that said, 'Kill.'"

—Cynthia Lennon

• •

• •

"They looked scruffy. . . . They dressed to shock. . . . Presley would appeal to John, because he could identify with him. Music of the 'underclass'. If you look at the early Beatles in their black leather jackets, they were Mods and Rockers. They were aggressively anti-. They weren't sure what they were against, but they were against it."

—Raymond Feather, who lived near John as a child

• •

When John Lennon was eighteen, he moved out of his aunt's house and into this building where he shared an apartment with his friend Stuart Sutcliffe.

then again when she died. The grief was too painful for him to face. To those around him, his reaction seemed almost inhumanly cold.

Despite his personal problems, though, he threw himself into his music. By the time he left art school two years later in July 1960, music had taken over John's life completely. The group he had formed in 1957 with Paul McCartney had finally begun to mature.

After many changes in the lineup, the group had brought in Stuart Sutcliffe on bass guitar along with a thirty-six-year-old drummer, Tommy Moore. They had played hundreds of times in small clubs and cafés in Liverpool. Technically, they showed fast progress, but were not yet confident enough to perform many of their own compositions. Instead, they played songs written by their heroes, notably the great Buddy Holly.

On a personal level, John's relationship with Cynthia had blossomed, despite disapproval from Cynthia's parents. John had moved out of Aunt Mimi's

house early in 1959 and now shared a place with his friend Stuart Sutcliffe.

John's music group changed its name on a regular basis, but by early 1960, it had settled on "The Silver Beatles." Although they failed one record company audition after another, they managed to secure a tour of Scotland as the backing band for a little-known singer named Johnny Gentle. It was their first taste of the music scene outside of their native Liverpool.

The tour was a very low-key affair, and the group treated it more as a vacation than work, but it was good experience and set them up for a more promising project that came their way soon after. They were invited to travel to Hamburg, Germany, and to take up a residency at a nightclub.

Hamburg

By August 1960, when John and his group left for Germany, they had shortened their name to "The Beatles." Before they went, they had to replace Tommy Moore, who had left after the tour of Scotland. His place was taken by Pete Best.

The Beatles' residency was at a sleazy club, the Kaiserkeller, on a street called the Reeperbahn. Then, as now, the Reeperbahn was in the middle of Hamburg's red-light district, home to drug dealers and other shady characters. It was also the heart of the city's jazz and pop music.

The first four-month stay in Hamburg completely changed the group. It turned the members from a band of amateurish college boys into a tight-knit professional-sounding pop group.

Yet, playing in Hamburg was an uncomfortable experience. They were paid very little and had to perform long sets that went on until the early hours of the morning. The audiences were violent and often smashed the furniture and leapt onto the stage at the end of the session. All the band members shared one room in a dingy apartment, where they slept during the day and worked at night. For John and the others, though, it was the most exciting thing they had ever done. This, they felt, was "real life," a genuine "rock and roll" existence. The

Beatles played in Hamburg for four and a half hours during the week and six hours over the weekends for more than one hundred nights, one after the other. They survived on cheap food, alcohol, and drugs.

Trademark

It was in Hamburg that the Beatles met an art student named Astrid Kirchherr, who struck up a close friendship with all five Beatles and fell in love with Stuart Sutcliffe. Astrid will always be remembered as the person who created the "Beatles hairstyle," the mop-top that would become one of the group's trademarks and was adopted by countless young men the world over just a few years later. Stuart Sutcliffe was the first to agree to have his hair cut, and John Lennon the last. Always rebellious, independent, and against any form of uniformity, John thought the haircut was laughable, but he was eventually persuaded when the others (except for Pete Best) adopted the style. When the group took the stage at the Kaiserkeller one night, the tiny German audience became the first to see the new look of the Beatles, a style that would soon be one of the ingredients that propelled the group to superstardom.

This trip to Hamburg was cut short when the Beatles were accused of breach of contract. This was followed by a report that George Harrison was underage, and then, Paul McCartney and Pete Best were evicted from their apartment. In total disarray, the Beatles made their way back to Liverpool individually, but Stuart Sutcliffe decided to stay in Hamburg to be with Astrid.

The Cavern Club

They arrived in Liverpool three weeks before Christmas in 1960. Life in his hometown struck John as a huge anticlimax after the excitement of Hamburg.

He wasted little time, however; he was determined to get things moving again for the group. News of their great reception in Hamburg had reached Liverpool ahead of them and people wanted to hear them play. Through a network of contacts and fans in the city,

"The Beatles as a pop group were very different to anything which had been before as idols of the teenager—Sinatra or any of them. They were . . . purposefully not respectable and slightly anti-establishment. Slightly James Dean."

—Raymond Feather, who lived near John as a child

John managed to secure some dates for the group at the Cavern Club.

The Cavern was a dimly lit, smoky jazz club in the middle of Liverpool. Musical styles changed rapidly during those years, and jazz was being gradually replaced by pop music. The manager of the Cavern wanted to showcase new young talent in the pop world.

The Beatles made their first appearance at the Cavern on March 21, 1961. John and Paul shared the lead vocals and played guitars—John played the rhythm on a six-string and Paul played the electric four-string bass guitar. George and Pete played guitar and drums. All of them wore black leather. It was to be the beginning of a two-and-a-half-year residency at the club, where they would eventually perform 292 times.

It was only the group's optimism and determination that kept them together, though. They found it increasingly difficult to make progress. They still failed record company auditions on a regular basis and had to rely on live performances to make a living and to improve their music.

The Beatles performed at the Cavern Club in Liverpool in the early 1960s. Here, John Lennon stands between his band mates and another musician.

This building now stands at the site of the Cavern Club, where the Beatles met their first manager, Brian Epstein.

A lucky break

One day in October 1961, a young man entered a Liverpool music shop and asked for the single "My Bonnie" by a group named the Beatles. The shop owner, a young man by the name of Brian Epstein, had never heard of the record, but promised that he would hunt it down and order it. During the next few weeks, several other people came into the shop and requested the same song. Puzzled, Epstein decided to find out more about the group. It was then that he discovered they were local boys and that they played regularly at the Cavern Club. His curiosity got the better of him and Epstein decided to visit the Cavern in November.

Instantly charmed both by the music and the look of the group on stage, he knew right away that he wanted to manage the Beatles and guide their future. Within a few days, he arranged to meet the group, and by December 3, 1961, he had become their manager.

The turning point

The arrival of Brian Epstein changed everything for John Lennon and the Beatles. John Lennon had drive and ambition, and together with Paul McCartney, his skill as a writer was maturing, but he did not have the organizational talent and business sense to manage the group. Fortunately for them, Brian Epstein did.

Epstein caught the group at just the right moment. It is probably no exaggeration to say that the Beatles would never have become world famous without this quiet, unassuming man to guide them through the cut-throat world of the music business.

The first thing that Epstein did was to tidy up the group's appearance. This immediately caused a clash with John. Epstein had a very conventional fashion sense and John resisted any attempt to stereotype him and his band to look like all the other groups of the time. To him, the group was a rough and ready, hard-hitting rock-and-roll band that did not conform to anything but its own ideas. The more conventional Paul sided with Epstein and there began an ongoing battle with Epstein and McCartney on one side and Lennon and Harrison on the other.

Finally, a compromise was reached when John agreed to their new manager's suggestion that the members of the band wear suits—later known as "Beatle suits." He insisted that they keep their long hair, however. John also kept his acts of rebellion, such as keeping his tie loosened and his top button undone when the group played live.

Epstein realized that the Beatles needed to project a strong, unified image. As he began to formulate his grand plans for the group, they continued to play at the Cavern, where they perfected their act and sharpened their musical style. They played all over England, not always with much success. At one gig, only eighteen people turned up.

Early in 1962, the Beatles made some of their first demonstration recordings, which Epstein took to every record company in London in an attempt to secure the group a recording contract. He was totally

In the early 1960s, the Beatles often performed for very small audiences.

By August 1962, the Beatles had their permanent lineup. From left to right, the musicians were George Harrison, Ringo Starr, Paul McCartney, and John Lennon.

unsuccessful. One after the other, the record companies turned the group down.

The pain of grief

In April 1962, the Beatles were invited to open the Star Club in Hamburg. It was a prestigious job and a sign that the group's reputation had begun to spread.

The group arrived at Hamburg airport to be met by a distraught Astrid Kirchherr. Astrid stared at John and said, "Stuart's dead, John. He's gone."

John's reaction was to burst into hysterical laughter. His words to Astrid were, "Make your decision. You either die with him or you go on living your life." It summed up John Lennon's philosophy of life perfectly, but deep beneath the surface, he felt the pain of grief.

John made sure that they still played at the club that night, as planned. The show was a great success, and the Beatles ended up staying in Hamburg for seven weeks.

Contract

Meanwhile, back in England, Epstein had finally managed to persuade a record company, EMI, to take on the Beatles. He secured the contract on May 9, 1962, and the group signed it on June 4, within days of their return to England.

From that moment on, things moved incredibly quickly. Two days after they signed the contract, John and the others were placed in Abbey Road Studios, London, for their first recording session.

John, Paul, George, and Ringo

A key ingredient in Brian Epstein's success with EMI was a young producer, George Martin. The two men got along immediately, and it was through this relationship that Epstein secured the Beatles' deal.

At first, George Martin was unsure about the songs Lennon and McCartney had written. He thought that they showed promise, but that their craft needed considerable improvement. It was only after their first recording session at Abbey Road Studios, and when he got to know them personally, that Martin recognized the potential of their talent. The first recording session was really seen as a trial run to discover what the group could do.

EMI was not happy with the band's drummer, Pete Best. They thought that he did not fit in with the other three stylistically and that the group should replace him.

John, Paul and George had no choice. If they were to carry on with their careers at EMI, then Pete Best would have to go. So, on August 16, the drummer, who had been with them for more than two years, was asked to leave. Two days later, another young drummer from Liverpool was recruited. His name was Ringo Starr.

The Beatles' first single, "Love Me Do," was released on October 5, 1962. Although it only entered the national chart at number forty-eight and finally reached number seventeen, EMI considered it a promising start, and further recording sessions were booked up for the end of the year.

Marriage

Meanwhile, John's personal life was changing as radically as his musical career. On a visit to his girlfriend, Cynthia, in Liverpool during August 1962, he had received some earth-shattering news. Cynthia was particularly quiet that evening, and John asked her if anything was wrong.

"I've been to the doctor's," she told him. "I'm pregnant."

In 1962, the socially acceptable thing to do was for John and Cynthia to get married. John did not hesitate. After he heard the news that Cynthia was expecting a baby, John immediately proposed. Cynthia accepted.

When Aunt Mimi received the news, she was shocked. She had not known that John and Cynthia's relationship was so serious. The wedding day was set for August 23, 1962, but Aunt Mimi refused to attend.

Brian Epstein took care of everything. He organized the ceremony, acted as best man, arranged for a reception, and booked cars and flowers.

In 1962, the Beatles signed a record contract. Their first single, "Love Me Do," was a strong start for the band.

• •

"When the Beatles were depressed, thinking the group was going nowhere . . . I'd say, 'Where are we going, fellas?' and they'd say, 'To the top, Johnny!' And I'd say, 'Where's that, fellas?' And they'd say, 'To the toppermost of the poppermost!' and I'd say 'Right' and we'd all cheer up."

—John Lennon

• •

25

Beatlemania!

After their first exposure to the general public with "Love Me Do" in 1962 and a television appearance in January 1963, the Beatles became an almost overnight success. In February, the group began its first tour around Great Britain. It was during this tour that what became known as Beatlemania began. Young fans started to follow the group around the country wherever they played. They mobbed the group as they emerged from their shows and pursued them for autographs. They screamed loudly throughout the Beatles' performances. Through press coverage and television, news of Beatlemania reached the public. A huge wave of publicity for the Beatles had begun.

Above: Beatles fans scream in excitement.

Opposite: Press coverage and television shows made the Beatles an overnight success.

A number one

The Beatles released a single called "Please, Please Me" in January 1963. It soared straight up the British charts and reached the number-one position in March 1963.

The Beatles had really made it.

For John, it was a dream come true. Ever since he had first heard Elvis Presley on the radio at Menlove Avenue, seven years earlier, he had dreamed about becoming a famous musician. Now here he was, at the age of twenty-two, with his own composition at the top of the British singles charts and his group the most successful in the country. This was only the beginning. The group recorded its first album during one eleven-hour session. By the end of it, John's voice was raw, which only added to the appeal of the final song, "Twist and Shout." They called the album *Please, Please Me*, and by May 1963, it was number one on the album charts.

Please, Please Me was a unique album for the time. Until then, nearly all pop records were performed by solo singers or groups who were not involved with the writing or arranging of their songs. They merely sang other people's arrangements and lyrics. On *Please, Please Me*, however, there were no less than eight Lennon-McCartney originals, a monumental achievement for a pop group of the time. It was also recorded quickly to capture the live sound of the group that was so successful.

With the release of the album, John Lennon and Paul McCartney were immediately recognized as great songwriters as well as singers and performers. Their songs were a breath of fresh air compared to the old ballads and sentimental songs of the era. The Beatles, John and Paul in particular, were viewed as a startling new force in the world of popular music. They had everything. The group consisted of four good-looking young men, they were great live performers, and they wrote their own catchy, memorable songs. As early as the summer of 1963, it was clear that great success lay ahead. They simply had to carry on the way they had started, guided by the charming and energetic Brian Epstein and the magical partnership of John and Paul.

As John's career took off, his first son was born on April 8, 1963. Cynthia and John named the baby Julian. John was not there for the birth; since the Beatles were in the middle of an extensive tour that

crisscrossed Great Britain. It was not until three days later that John had enough free time to travel to Liverpool to see his newborn son.

1963 was definitely the year of the Beatles in England. Never in the history of entertainment had a pop group reached such heights of fame as the group had so rapidly achieved. Beatlemania reached its hysterical peak during that year in Britain.

To young people, the group was the coolest thing since Elvis Presley and, in 1963, these fans put the group into the record books. The Beatles' third single, "From Me To You," went to number one almost instantly—as did every other record they released that year. In August, the band released "She Loves You," and in December, "I Want To Hold Your Hand." Both of these singles sold more than 1 million copies each in Great Britain alone.

Because of their good looks and talent, fans saw the Beatles as a fresh new force in popular music.

"Outstanding composers"

"I Want To Hold Your Hand" is estimated to have sold more than 12 million copies worldwide. When it was released in the United States, it was reported to be selling at the rate of ten thousand copies an hour in New York alone.

In 1963, the Beatles' first album, *Please, Please Me*, had been number one on the album chart for a staggering thirty weeks and was only knocked out of that position by their second album, *With the Beatles*, which was released in November. On December 27, *The Times* newspaper described John Lennon and Paul McCartney as "the outstanding English composers of 1963."

The Beatles had Great Britain and the rest of Europe in a euphoria of Beatlemania. Their next target had to be America. Although their records sold well in the United States, it was a difficult market for foreign acts

to break into. Other groups had failed miserably. The Beatles had to wonder whether they would be able to make the same powerful impact on the United Sates as they had in Europe.

Success

When the Beatles flew into Kennedy Airport, New York, on February 7, 1964, they were met by huge crowds eager to see the British lads. The Beatles could hardly believe it. During 1963, the influence of American pop musicians had dwindled to almost nothing. Throughout the late 1950s and early 1960s, nearly all pop music was derived from or performed by American singers and writers. With the arrival of the Beatles, though, everything changed. Their "Englishness," so evident in their lyrics and in the way they sang, as well as the fresh sound of their music, was to revolutionize the pop music scene throughout the world.

John Lennon—film star

After a short tour of the East Coast of the United States, an endless stream of television and radio inter-views, award ceremonies, and gala lunches, the group was back in Great Britain to start on its next project, a movie entitled *A Hard Day's Night*.

A Hard Day's Night was made in black and white and was a simple story that revolved around the crazy world in which the Beatles had found themselves. The flimsy plot was the hectic schedule of the Beatles' new lives. Throughout the movie, they rush from trains to cars to shows and hotel rooms, mobbed by fans. They try desperately to lead something like a life of their own amid the hype and excitement of their huge fame.

The idea for *A Hard Day's Night* came from a chance remark John Lennon made to a journalist when he was asked what he thought of Sweden, a country in which the group had recently performed. John's reply was typically dry. "Oh, it was a room and a car, and a car and a room, and a plane and a car."

The main problem with the shooting of the movie was the fact that everywhere the Beatles went, they

Above: In February 1964, the Beatles gave their first U.S. concert in Washington, D.C.

Left: In March 1964, the Beatles began filming their first movie, A Hard Day's Night.

were mobbed by fans. As soon as news got out that the group was in town, hundreds of people would turn up and disrupt the filming. This meant that the film crew could only manage to snatch a few minutes of filming at any particular location before the group had to be ushered away by police. The movie had become a true reflection of the Beatles' lives.

In the midst of it all, John was becoming fed up with the Beatlemania craze. The band's members had all become victims of their own success and had no real identity of their own. They were simply the four lovable mop-tops.

John Lennon—writer

1964 was also the year John Lennon became a best-selling author with his book, *In His Own Write*.

When John was invited to collect the best of his nonsense poems and bizarre drawings for publication, it was obvious that the book would sell extremely well, since it was written by a Beatle, still the publishers were

astonished by its instant, huge success. *In His Own Write* sold more than one hundred thousand copies in its first print run and, overnight, John Lennon was celebrated as a great new literary find and comic genius.

From then on, John was no longer seen as a mere pop star. His writing showed intelligence and a natural wit. Comparisons were made between John's work and that of great English writers Edward Lear and Lewis Carroll. The literary critics loved John's work.

Help!

1964 ended with the Beatles at the pinnacle of their fame and global adulation. They had conquered America, sold millions of records, and with the premiere of *A Hard Day's Night* in

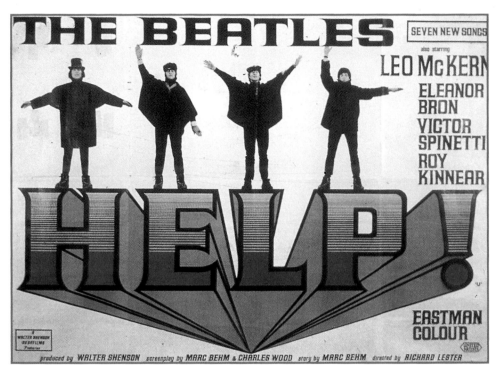

THE BEATLES

SEVEN NEW SONGS

also starring

LEO McKERN
ELEANOR BRON
VICTOR SPINETTI
ROY KINNEAR

HELP!

EASTMAN COLOUR

produced by *WALTER SHENSON*   screenplay by *MARC BEHM & CHARLES WOOD*   story by *MARC BEHM*   directed by *RICHARD LESTER*

The Beatles' second film, Help!, *was filmed in 1965 and was an immediate hit when it was released in August.*

July, had successfully made the transition to film. Through it all, they also retained their dominance of the pop scene. In 1964, the Beatles were voted in a survey as Great Britain's Most Popular Tourist Attraction.

Early in 1965, the group made its second movie, a far more ambitious project entitled *Help!*. Looking back on it, the music for the movie, and in particular, the title track written by John, was a clear sign that, on a personal level, things were not going so well for him. The lyrics "Help! I need somebody! Help! Not just anybody" came like a cry from John.

John Lennon had always been a restless character who forever looked forward to his next project and further glories. He was never content to sit back and simply enjoy past achievements. The problem for John Lennon was simple. As far as he could see, he had made it, he had done it all, and there were no other challenges.

The shooting of *Help!* coincided with what John called his "fat Elvis" period. He was plump and unhappy, despite his enormous wealth and fame.

At this time, the group became involved with marijuana. It is well known that the Beatles had been introduced to "pep-pills" in Hamburg and that they used them to keep alert through exhausting sets and to give them a "high" when mixed with alcohol. It was not until 1965 that drugs became a habit, however.

John smoked marijuana to get out of his depressed mood and because he believed, rightly or wrongly, that people should try everything at least once. It was in his nature to experiment, and with the Beatles' wealth and fame, marijuana was easily available.

Meanwhile, praise continued to come the Beatles' way. In June, John's second book, *A Spaniard in the Works*, was published. It immediately enjoyed the same huge success as his first volume. In August, the album *Help!* was released and shot straight to the top and, in the same month, the movie was premiered in New York to rave reviews by critics and the public.

The group returned to America and completed a national tour, which included a performance at the enormous Shea Stadium in New York. The screams of the fans drowned out every note the band played.

Royal approval

Above all the praise and fan worship, probably the most important honor the Beatles received in 1965 was their inclusion in the Queen's Birthday Honors List. They were also made Members of the British Empire (MBEs), an honorary British title. John felt unsure about the MBE. He would have rather refused it, but was persuaded to accept the award at the insistence of Paul, George, Ringo, and band manager Brian Epstein.

John always believed that his music and lyrics should come first. Fame and money enabled him to do what he loved and he was grateful for his success. At the same time, he resented the fact that the Beatles had to compromise so much to make their more recent

Above: The Beatles, in a film still from Help!*, were at the peak of their success in the mid-1960s.*

Below: Lennon wrote the title track for the film.

achievements. He once told a reporter that the Beatles had stopped being a real band after their days in Hamburg.

"We're more popular than Jesus!"

1966 turned out to be another year of great change for twenty-six-year-old John Lennon and the Beatles. It was a year in which John, in particular, ran into one controversy after another and almost destroyed the Beatles forever.

In view of John's feelings about the huge success and craziness of his life as a Beatle, it seemed that the situation had to change. The way that this was to occur surprised everyone, however.

In March 1966, Lennon gave an interview to a London newspaper in which he made a passing comment that he thought the Beatles were now more popular than Jesus Christ. What he meant by the statement was that, if the world were taken as a whole, there were quite literally more people who had heard of the Beatles than there were Christians. Little did he realize what an uproar the comment would cause.

In Great Britain, Lennon's remark went unnoticed. The public was used to such statements from the most outspoken and cocky of the Beatles. Five months later, though, on the eve of a major U.S. tour, the interview was repeated in an American magazine. Within days, religious people throughout the country had picked up on the remark and were deeply shocked.

American media were outraged and leapt on the story, which was portrayed as the ultimate in blasphemy. Radio stations in the southern states immediately banned Beatles' records. In a number of American cities, the public burned huge piles of Beatles' records.

John Lennon always found it difficult to apologize to anyone. He saw it as a sign of weakness. The only person who could ever solicit a "sorry" from him was his aunt Mimi. In the wake of this new crisis in the Beatles' career, though, he had no option but to apologize publicly at a press conference held in Chicago. The Beatles' very career was on the line.

It was yet another blow to Lennon's already frail

emotional state. In response, he turned even more to the blind comfort of alcohol and drugs, but even this was to prove insufficient. The near-catastrophe of the controversy brought him to the realization that something had to change. "After the Beatles' last tour," he said, "which was the one where the Ku Klux Klan were burning Beatles' records and I was held up as a satanist or something, then we decided, 'No more touring, that's enough of that.'" He decided that he could no longer continue with the endless touring undertaken by the group ever since their first appearances in Hamburg more than six years earlier.

The end of an era

John was not alone in his desire to end the merry-go-round of tours and the ceaseless pressure of the Beatles' existence as a live band. George Harrison was tired of live performances, and shared Lennon's view

As depicted in this film still from A Hard Day's Night, *crowds met the Beatles wherever they traveled.*

Above: The 1967 Beatles'
album Sgt. Pepper's Lonely
Hearts Club Band became
one of the most influential
albums in music history.

that the group should instead put all their efforts
into recording.

Paul McCartney and Brian Epstein were horrified
by the idea. McCartney always thrived as a perform-
ing musician and loved the excitement. To him, it
was an essential part of being in a group. For
Epstein, Lennon's decision was disastrous. If the
Beatles did not perform live, there remained little for
him to do as manager. Lennon would not budge,
though. He needed a change and did not care whose
feelings he hurt.

The Beatles played what was to be their last-ever
performance at Candlestick Park in San Francisco,
California, on August 29, 1966. The group contin-

ued to work solely as recording artists, and some of their most artistically successful compositions were written and recorded in this period. Since they were no longer under constant pressure to deliver new albums twice a year and to play an endless series of concerts, they could concentrate on their studio skills and branch out into experimental areas of music. As the world of pop culture changed rapidly during the late

The Beatles, photographed here around the time of the release of Sgt. Pepper's Lonely Hearts Club Band*, performed their last live concert in August 1966.*

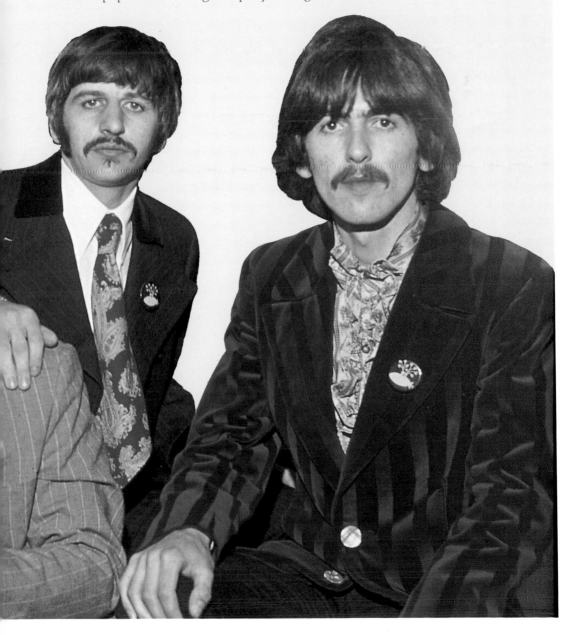

summer of 1966, the Beatles were again to prove they were still quite able to stay one step ahead of everyone else.

John Lennon's decision to bring an end to the old-style Beatles brought an abrupt end to an era beloved by the public of both Great Britain and America. As Brian Epstein had feared, the decision also made his work as manager almost unnecessary.

Yoko Ono and Sgt. Pepper

John's life with Cynthia had been going through a very rocky period for some time. Cynthia refused to support John's involvement with drugs, and as Lennon's marijuana habit got worse, his relationship with Cynthia began to crumble. Added to this was the fact that he had begun to grow increasingly restless with his life as a Beatle and bored with his marriage. He wanted to share his life with someone he considered more dynamic and in tune with his own unusual, rebellious personality.

On November 9, he met that person—a small, dark-haired Japanese artist named Yoko Ono—at an art gallery in London. At the same time that John began this new relationship, the Beatles were spending all their time in the recording studio, once again moving into areas of music never before explored by pop musicians.

Their new sound, which later became known as psychedelic music, was influenced by the drugs with which they had now all become heavily involved. They started to take a lot of the hallucinogenic drug LSD, or acid, which, they felt, enhanced their imaginations. LSD became known as a "mind-expanding" drug, despite the very serious dangers it posed to those who used it.

It was the age of "Flower Power," when thousands of young people genuinely believed that they could change the world simply through love. During 1967, "the summer of love," as it became known, as many people experimented with LSD, a new drug culture emerged. The Beatles were at the forefront of the movement, and John Lennon, more than anyone else, was seen as the new leader of this youth movement.

These new ideas were expressed in the Beatles' music of the time. Songs such as "Strawberry Fields Forever" and "Penny Lane" set the stage for what was to become the year of love and harmony. "Living is easy with eyes closed, misunderstanding all you see. It's getting hard to be someone but it all works out. It doesn't really matter much to me," said the lyrics of "Strawberry Fields." In both of these songs, the Beatles used a variety of exotic instruments to complement the usual guitar, bass, and drums of the traditional pop song. They had begun this trend on their 1965 album *Rubber Soul*, which had included the use of the sitar, piano, and organ.

In 1968, the movie Yellow Submarine *featured the Beatles as cartoon characters.*

43

Above: The late 1960s hippie movement was reflected in psychedelic art and fashion.

In June 1967, the Beatles released the totally revolutionary album *Sgt. Pepper's Lonely Hearts Club Band.* It became one of the best-selling albums of all time and certainly the most influential "pop" record ever recorded. *Sgt. Pepper* is a truly inspired album, and it blends Lennon and McCartney's new lease of life as composers with the technical wizardry of their producer, George Martin. On this album, the Beatles covered the full range of experimental pop music of the day. George Martin used special studio effects, such as

echo, and a lot of devices to alter voices, guitars, keyboard instruments, and drums. It was this that gave the album its distinctive atmosphere.

Sgt. Pepper put the Beatles into a new league of composers. They had fused pop music with the influence of modern classical composers such as Pierre Boulez and Stockhausen. At the same time, though, they had maintained a grip on the accessible "popular" musical form that was built around the three-minute pop song. It was probably the group's greatest achievement.

Above left: John Lennon embraced the new drug culture and was seen by many as a leader of the youth movement.

Above: Vivid psychedelic patterns were even painted onto people's bodies as an expression of the "Flower Power" movement.

In 1967, John Lennon bought this Rolls Royce and had it painted with psychedelic colors.

All you need is love

By the summer of 1967, Flower Power had reached its peak. The Beatles performed their latest single, "All You Need is Love," on a worldwide television broadcast to an estimated audience of 400 million. The song's lyrics perfectly summed up the peace-loving mood of the time: "All you need is love, All you need is love, All you need is love, love, Love is all you need."

As was typical of John Lennon, his interest in the effects of drugs on his mind had now diminished and he had begun to look elsewhere for the same mind-expanding effects. Through George Harrison's interest in Eastern religion, the whole group became fascinated with meditation. The group became disciples of the Indian guru the Maharishi Mahesh Yogi, under whom they studied meditation.

Meditation is a technique used to bring a person relaxation and to enable a greater communication with the subconscious mind. The Beatles, and especially George Harrison and John Lennon, believed that this would help them find peace and happiness and to be more creative.

John was very influenced by what he learned at this time, and it has been said that he gained many of his peace-loving ideals from this period in his life. Others attribute these changes to the influence of Yoko Ono and the side-effects of excessive drug use. If nothing else, meditation certainly had an effect on his songwriting, but it undoubtedly played a part in the creation of the psychedelic Beatles sound of the late 1960s.

By this time, Lennon's relationship with his wife, Cynthia, was rapidly decaying as his love for Yoko Ono grew. In late August, he set off with the other members of the group and their partners for a meditation weekend in Wales. Through a series of mishaps, Cynthia was left behind in London and only managed to join them later. For Cynthia, this summed up what was happening to their relationship. Although she knew she would get to Wales, Cynthia was aware of more than just missing the train. As she put it, "I just felt so sad that this is symbolic of our life now, you know. It's like 'I'm getting off at this station' and it was pretty true after that." This may have seemed like the worst that could happen, but there was a terrible disaster in store for that weekend.

Still suffering from the effects of his beloved Beatles' decision not to tour any longer, Brian Epstein became deeply depressed, and on August 27, he was found dead in his Belgravia apartment. When John and the others heard the news, they were devastated. Epstein had made the Beatles. Their musical success lay in the craftsmanship of John and Paul's songs, but it was their manager, Brian Epstein, who had raised them from playing in dingy bars along with hundreds of other hopefuls to the soaring heights of global fame.

With Brian Epstein's death, something died in the Beatles. It was as though an essential ingredient had been removed from the recipe that made the group what they were. The Beatles were never the same again. From 1967 on, their career went into a gradual decline.

The magic is lost

People have often guessed at why the Beatles were so incredibly successful. The only clear answer must be that they each had a great deal of talent and were in the right place at the right time. What is important is not so much the quickness of their success, but the fact that the group continued to be successful for the better part of a decade.

In many ways, the Beatles were very traditional. They were a four-piece, all-male group that played conventional instruments and sang songs about love. What made them unique was a combination of things: the strength of their melodies, their ability to merge vocal tunes with the right backing, the quality of John and Paul's voices, and their unmatched vocal harmonies. They were also good-looking, had a great sense of fun, and above all, they were able to repeat their winning formula over and over without ever sounding repetitive. Without Brian Epstein, however, somehow the magic of the Beatles was lost.

John Lennon and the rest of the Beatles visited the Maharishi Mahesh Yogi in India in 1967.

Lost direction

The Beatles had lost their direction. They still made hit albums and continued to be always one step ahead of other pop groups throughout the world, but it was only a matter of time before the cracks would begin to show.

Meanwhile, in November 1968, Lennon's marriage to Cynthia ended in divorce. At the same time, John made his love for Yoko Ono public.

This was not the only personal change that occurred. By 1968, the relationship between the Beatles' key songwriting elements, John and Paul, had exhausted itself. They had outgrown each other and both needed to move on to other projects.

Once John had met Yoko Ono, who was an off-beat, modern artist, John found that he wanted to explore avenues outside the limits of the Beatles, their fame, and all that they stood for. For Paul's part, John's refusal to play live restricted him too much, and he needed to find challenges outside the close-knit group of the Beatles.

The end finally came in 1970, but in reality, the group had not played together for many months. Lawyers were employed to sort out their affairs and the public announcement was made that the Beatles were no more. "There could never be another Beatles, never," grieved fans.

A walk on the wild side

Following the breakup of the Beatles, John went through a wild period in which the general public watched the ex-Beatle with growing astonishment. Many believed he had finally crossed the line between genius and madman.

After his marriage to Cynthia ended, John had married Yoko in Gibraltar in March 1969. To coincide with this major personal change, he began a highly political phase of his life. The most important campaign was John and Yoko's famous public demonstrations for global peace.

John and Yoko spent their honeymoon in an hotel

Opposite top: John and Cynthia Lennon visited the Maharishi in early 1968. During that time, John Lennon studied transcendental meditation.

Opposite below: The 1968 film Yellow Submarine *was a great success. In this still photo from the film, cartoon George and John (right) talk to the captain of the submarine.*

. . . .

"The bigger we got, the more unreality we had to face. . . . It happened bit by bit, gradually, until this complete craziness is surrounding you, and you're doing exactly what you don't want to do with people you can't stand— the people you hated when you were ten."

—John Lennon

. . . .

49

in Amsterdam, Holland. As an antiwar demonstration, they stayed in bed for a whole week with the doors open to all press and cameras. The posters on the walls and windows shouted, "Grow your Hair," "Bed Peace," and "Hair Peace." They sent acorns to world leaders and asked for them to be planted as symbols of peace. They appeared on television talk shows inside bags. This, they claimed, was "total communication." They did not want people to confuse their message for peace with the shade of their skin or the length of their hair, and this could not happen when viewers could only see the bags.

For a public sickened by war and death and tragic Third World famine, the antics of John and Yoko were recognized as invaluable contributions to the peace movement—the power of the publicity they attracted was immense. Many thought the way they sought that publicity, however, was crazy.

Above: Although John Lennon appeared in the film How I Won the War, *he strongly disagreed with the involvement of the United States in the Vietnam War.*

Amid all these attention-grabbing stunts, John Lennon never once forgot where his real talent lay. In the summer of 1969, he and Yoko formed a new group called the Plastic Ono Band.

The group's first performance was a rather chaotic affair at a huge concert in Toronto, Canada. John and Yoko hired a number of famous musicians, including the guitarist Eric Clapton. After a few rehearsals, one of which took place during the flight to Canada, the makeshift group played to a vast and appreciative audience.

The performance showcased John's new composition, "Give Peace a Chance." It became a new anthem for global youth and played its part in an attempt to defuse the volatile atmosphere of aggression of the time. It is a song that, like nearly all of the Beatles' compositions, has lasted and is re-released periodically to repeated chart success.

Above: John Lennon and Yoko Ono demonstrated for peace from their bed (top) as a form of nonviolent protest against the war in Vietnam.

Lennon's political activism made it difficult for him to establish official residency in the United States.

To the amazement of the British public, in November 1969, John returned the MBE, which he had not really wanted to accept in the first place. The incident caused almost as much international outcry as the granting of the award four years earlier.

Further political activity marked the last months of the decade, and many of John and Yoko's songs were focused on topical subjects. For example, "Angela" was recorded for radical African American activist Angela Davis. John and Yoko also appeared at numerous demonstrations.

A week before Christmas, 1969, the couple financed a set of huge posters that simply said, "War Is Over! If you want it. Happy Christmas from John and Yoko." The posters appeared on gigantic billboards in eleven cities across the world and presented the U.S. government with the most obvious statement against American involvement in the Vietnam War that anyone could ask for.

As the last days of "the Beatles decade" ticked away, John received further recognition when one of the television channels in Great Britain transmitted a show called "Man of the Decade," in which John was profiled as one of the three most influential people of the decade. The other two were of John F. Kennedy and the Chinese leader Mao Tse-tung. Little more than seven years after the Beatles' first single, John Lennon had acquired global recognition for his achievements.

"Imagine"

The next few years of John Lennon's life marked a period of frenetic activity. He and Yoko were still passionately involved in politics, but it was also a time in which John's musical output was even more publicly visible.

In July 1971, he recorded what was to become perhaps his most famous song, "Imagine." The lyrics of "Imagine" are hopeful, claiming that love can conquer all. "Imagine" is a song that makes an abrupt departure from the usual themes of most pop music. Instead of romanticizing personal relationships, the lyrics speak of universal unity and peace. For many people, it became a banner, a symbol of their hopes and ideals.

Soon after John and Yoko left Great Britain, "Imagine" was released. In many ways, Lennon was never very comfortable in his home country. He felt, quite rightly, that the British public viewed him as a crazy, rich, and spoiled pop star who whined about world peace but lived a luxurious lifestyle that he only partly deserved.

In New York, he felt more relaxed and respected. Great Britain still yearned for the old-style Beatles, the lovable mop-tops, but John Lennon had moved on. He wanted to be appreciated as the artist he had always wanted to become and saw New York as the only place where he could establish a new life for himself. So, in September 1971, he and Yoko set up home there and made plans for the future. John Lennon never returned to Great Britain.

Legal battles

For John Lennon, the first half of the 1970s marked an era in which he was simultaneously engaged in two big legal battles. One of these was his five-year fight to remain in the United States, and the other was the legal tussle over the breakup of the Beatles.

John found it very difficult to obtain a green card, the official certification that allows a person to have permanent residence in the United States. His problem had its origins in a drug offense that dated back to 1968. Many people, however, believe that the real reason for the government's resistance stemmed from John and Yoko's political activity. The immigration battle continued, and it was not until July 1976 that Lennon could finally claim victory, when he received his green card from the U.S. Immigration Department.

Meanwhile, the legal wrangles over the Beatles' fortune continued on both sides of the Atlantic. The Beatles' finances were a mess, principally because of bad management after Brian Epstein's death. In May 1968, the four members of the Beatles had formed the disastrously ill-conceived Apple Corporation, which

John Lennon and Yoko Ono separated in 1973, soon after this photograph was taken.

• •

"The message is peace! You can protest about violence in many ways, and this is one. "

—John Lennon

• •

Above: John Lennon had a villa in Palm Beach, Florida (top), as well as an apartment in the luxurious Dakota Building (below) in New York.

was created to expand their ventures into fashion, design, and the promotion of budding artists. It had started with good intentions, but without the expert guidance of the Beatles' mentor, Brian Epstein, it had soon run into trouble. At one point, it was said to be losing the group thousands of pounds (British currency) a day. After the Beatles finally split up in 1970, their legal affairs became horribly tangled because Paul McCartney had employed one legal expert to sort things out, and John, George, and Ringo had hired another.

Things became even more complicated in 1973, when John fell into disagreements with the company fighting his case against Paul. The question of the Beatles' millions, the legal battles over Apple, and the dissolution of the Beatles in the courts did not take place until the beginning of 1977, almost seven years after the group had stopped playing together and the Lennon-McCartney partnership had fallen apart.

The big split

Throughout this turbulent period of legal wrangles and hard-fought court cases, John did not forget his music, nor did he slow his political activity. There was another personal crisis looming, though. In October 1973, John and Yoko split up. The reason for the breakup of their relationship has always been unclear. Whatever the cause, the news traveled around the world and made headlines everywhere.

One explanation was that Yoko felt that John needed some time on his own if she were to continue to live with him. She supposedly considered the split as a temporary event, designed to help John to change his ways.

Neither of them saw the separation as a permanent thing. That, however, did not diminish the pain and sense of loss felt by John. It was decided that he should move to Los Angeles with his secretary, May Pang, and Yoko would remain in New York to run their business affairs.

John took it very badly; he called it his "lost weekend" period. For nearly eighteen months, he remained in California and led a chaotic life, working furiously in the studio and suffering bouts of violent drunkenness.

Despite his emotional stress, the time he spent away from Yoko saw the release of some of his best work. One aspect of John's music that could never be taken away was his wonderful voice. He always hated the sound of his own voice, however, and tried to use every studio effect available to change it. Fortunately for the music business, the public did not agree with his feelings about his own vocals, and during his time in California, he wrote a series of hit songs.

He made many new friends and renewed old relationships during 1974. In particular, his collaborations with musicians Elton John and David Bowie helped him out of the dangerous lifestyle he had adopted. He released three excellent albums between 1973 and 1975.

The first was *Mind Games*, most of which was recorded in New York before his separation from Yoko. It was released in November 1973 and became an

John Lennon and Yoko Ono lived in New York in the 1970s.

instant hit. Next came *Walls and Bridges* in October 1974. This album included his first solo American number-one single, "Whatever Gets You Thru The Night." Then, in February 1975, the album of 1950s songs, *Rock 'n' Roll*, appeared.

Reunion

By January 1975, Yoko was ready to have John back. Within just a few weeks of their reunion, Yoko became pregnant.

At the beginning of 1975, Lennon was on the verge of yet another significant change in the direction of his life. He felt drained as a writer and musician and was rapidly losing interest in the music business. In June of that year, he made what was to be his final live performance on an American television show. He performed "Imagine" and "Slippin' and a Slidin'" from the *Rock 'n' Roll* album.

On October 9, John's thirty-fifth birthday, Yoko gave birth to a son named Sean. Yoko had experienced three miscarriages during their relationship, and John and Yoko were thrilled with the birth of Sean. It was this event that finally pushed John into a decision. After he played piano on Ringo Starr's latest solo album, *Rotogravure*, in April 1976, he decided to stop playing music altogether.

John decided to make the switch from internationally famous pop star to "house husband." He felt he needed an extended break from music and all that his career involved. For the next four-and-a-half years, he totally disappeared from the global pop music arena. With Yoko and Sean, he secluded himself in their luxurious apartment in the Dakota Building that overlooked Central Park on West 72nd Street, New York.

The second half of the 1970s was a peaceful time for John, and he thrived away from the chaotic atmosphere of the music business. He took occasional foreign solo trips to strengthen his independence and continually found different things to fill the void left by his departure from the career that had dominated his life.

1980

On one of his trips away from Yoko and Sean, John sailed his yacht, *Isis*, to Bermuda. While there, relaxed and happy, he began to write music again.

In August 1980, John and Yoko returned to work in a recording studio. The break from music had revitalized his interest, and the songs came easily to him. He felt ready to take on the music scene again. During August, songs that would eventually appear on his album *Double Fantasy* began to take shape and he and Yoko began to seriously organize their comeback.

To set the publicity machine into motion again, they lined up a series of interviews and began to look around for a suitable record company to release the new album. John had not renewed his contract with EMI when it had expired early in 1976, so he found a new home for his talent in a recently established label called Geffen Records.

October 1980 was the month of John's fortieth birthday and Sean's fifth. Yoko celebrated the event with a message of love sky-written over Manhattan. A little more than a month later, John's first album in more than five years was released. It was immediately received with rave reviews and was a huge commercial success. John Lennon was back in business.

Mark Chapman

December 8, 1980, began like any other day. It was winter in New York City, but unseasonably mild. John and Yoko spent the day at the Hit Factory, the recording studio where they had made the *Double Fantasy* album. They were at work on a new set of songs for another album and John was still in the full flush of a rediscovered creativity.

As he left for the studio early in the day, on his way to the car parked outside the Dakota Building, John signed an autograph for a fan who had been waiting for his hero to appear. John smiled at the young man, who clutched a copy of *Double Fantasy*. Then John jumped in beside Yoko as the car sped off to the studio. The fan's name was Mark Chapman.

In August 1980, John Lennon returned the studio to record music again. Here he shows his son Sean, age five, the studio's sound-mixing console.

JOHN LENNON SHOT DEAD

Gunned down by 'screwball' outside home as wife Yoko watches in horror

DRAMATIC COVERAGE: PAGES 2, 3, 4, 5, 31, 32, 33

Above: John Lennon's murder on December 8, 1980, was hard for many fans to believe.

Opposite top: John Lennon and Yoko Ono posed for this photo after Lennon's fortieth birthday. It was one of the last photos taken of them together.

Opposite below: Soon after Lennon's murder, crowds filled the streets in Liverpool as a final tribute to him.

After a long day recording, the couple left the studio late in the evening and were driven in a black limousine through Manhattan to the Dakota Building. The car pulled up outside at 10:49 P.M.

John stepped out of the car and headed for the building's entrance ahead of Yoko. He was listening to one of her songs, "Walking On Thin Ice." As he entered the archway that led to the building's doors, a voice came from the shadows a few feet away: "Mr. Lennon?"

John turned, and Mark Chapman shot five bullets from a .38 revolver into John Lennon's back and side at point-blank range.

The end

Suddenly, there was chaos in the foyer of the Dakota Building. John staggered up the six steps to the entrance and fell through the doors, where he collapsed on the floor just inside the entrance, blood gushing from the bullet wounds. Yoko screamed and rushed to him, shouting to the stunned doorman to call an ambulance.

Within two minutes, a police car arrived and two policemen had pinned Chapman against the wall, a few feet from where John lay in a pool of blood. When he realized that there was no time to wait for an ambulance to arrive, one of the police officers carried John Lennon to the squad car outside and rushed him to the nearest hospital, the Roosevelt on 58th Street. The hospital's major trauma team had been alerted in advance by a radio call from the police car.

The medical team battled to revive John, but it proved to be an impossible task. John Lennon was pronounced dead on arrival.

The world is stunned

The world was totally stunned by John Lennon's murder. To most people, he was seen as the embodiment of peace, a latter-day Mahatma Gandhi or Martin Luther King Jr. To his millions of fans throughout the world, as well as to those who did not care too much for his music, John Lennon's assassination was the senseless act of a madman. It was hardly believable. Radio stations throughout the world devoted the day to playing John Lennon's music, and for weeks after the shooting, thousands of fans besieged the Dakota Building, where they played a nonstop soundtrack of Lennon's music on tape recorders and transistor radios.

The day after the shooting, Lennon's murderer, Mark Chapman, was given a fifteen-minute hearing. He was sentenced to life imprisonment and incarcerated in the top-security Attica state prison.

John's murder devastated Yoko. If it had not been for her son, Sean, she probably would have found it impossible to continue. Over the following months, a quarter of a million sympathy letters arrived at the Dakota Building from all over the world, as well as tributes from the great and the humble of every continent.

Fans placed flowers and tokens of remembrance on the front gate of the Dakota Building soon after Lennon's murder.

Ten minutes' silence

John Lennon was cremated at Hartsdale Crematorium in New York State. On Sunday, December 14, 1980, a crowd of an estimated three hundred thousand people attended a memorial service in Central Park. Around the world a ten-minute silence was called and his millions of fans paid tribute to the man who had meant so much to generations of people. At 2:00 P.M., all radio and television transmissions were suspended for ten minutes and cities fell silent. In Great Britain, the three surviving Beatles mourned with the rest of the world, as did John's aunt Mimi and Lennon's hundreds of close personal friends.

John Lennon was not merely a great musician and composer, he was a great human being. He had his critics, and there have been many who, since his death, have tried to peel away what they see as the "Lennon myth." To many millions of people of all ages, however, John Lennon symbolized a sense of hope for the future.

If he had done nothing more than written great songs, such as "She Loves You," "Please, Please Me," and "Strawberry Fields Forever," he would have gone down as one of the greatest composers of all time. John Lennon achieved much more, though. With songs such as "Imagine" and "Give Peace a Chance," he showed that it was possible to question outdated values, to fight with words and music for what one believes in, to remain faithful to a deeply rooted faith in humankind, and to find some meaning in life. Madman or genius, with his insistent cry to "be yourself," John Lennon's music and his philosophy will continue to be an inspiration for all those who struggle for any kind of freedom, today and for generations to come.

Timeline

1940   October 9: John Winston Lennon is born to Julia and Freddy Lennon in Liverpool, England. Before his first birthday, John goes to live with his aunt Mimi and uncle George.

1945   September: John starts at Dovedale Primary School, Liverpool.

1952   September: Shortly before his twelfth birthday, John Lennon starts at Quarry Bank High School, Liverpool.

1955   June 5: John's uncle George dies suddenly.

1957   May: John forms his first group, the Quarry Men. He is the lead singer and chooses the band's material.
July 6: John Lennon and Paul McCartney meet at a church social, where the Quarry Men are playing. John and Paul start to play and write songs together.
September: John becomes a student at the Liverpool College of Art.

1958   February: George Harrison joins the Quarry Men.
July 15: John's mother, Julia Lennon, is killed in a road accident.

1960   John leaves college, and with his newly named group, the Beatles, goes to Hamburg, Germany, in August.

1961   March 21: The Beatles make their debut at the Cavern Club in Liverpool.
December 3: Brian Epstein becomes the Beatles' manager.

1962   April: The Beatles are invited to open the Star Club in Hamburg.
June 4: The Beatles sign a recording contract with EMI.
August 18: Ringo Starr joins the Beatles.
August 23: John Lennon and Cynthia Powell are married.
October 5: The Beatles release their first single, "Love Me Do."

1963   February: The Beatles start their first tour of Great Britain.
March 2: The Beatles' second single, "Please, Please Me," reaches number one.
April 8: John and Cynthia have a son, Julian.
May 4: The Beatles' first album, *Please, Please Me*, tops the charts.
November: The Beatles perform at the Royal Variety Show. The Beatles release "I Want to Hold Your Hand." An estimated twelve million copies are sold worldwide.

1964   February 7: The Beatles begin their first tour of the United States.
March 23: John Lennon publishes a selection of poetry and drawings called *In His Own Write*. It sells more than one hundred thousand copies in its first print run.
July 6: The Beatles' movie *A Hard Day's Night* premieres in London.

1965   June: John Lennon publishes his second book, *A Spaniard in the Works*.
July 29: The Beatles' second movie, *Help!*, has its world premiere in London.
October 26: The Beatles are awarded MBEs, presented by the queen at Buckingham Palace.

1966   August 29: The Beatles play their last live performance at Candlestick Park in San Francisco, California.
November 9: John Lennon meets Yoko Ono.

1967	The "summer of love" is celebrated and "Flower Power" is at its peak. The Beatles release "Strawberry Fields Forever," "Penny Lane," and "All You Need Is Love." John begins his antiwar campaign.
	June 1: The album *Sgt. Pepper's Lonely Hearts Club Band* is released.
	August 27: The Beatles' manager, Brian Epstein, dies.
1968	May: The Beatles set up the ill-fated Apple Corporation.
	November: John and Cynthia are divorced.
	November 28: John is found guilty of marijuana possession and is fined.
1969	March 20: John Lennon and Yoko Ono marry in Gibraltar. During their honeymoon, they stage a "bed-in" as a peace protest in an Amsterdam hotel room. John releases the single "Give Peace a Chance."
	November: John Lennon returns his MBE to the queen.
	December: On a television show in Great Britain, John is profiled as one of the three most influential people of the decade.
(1970)	April: The Beatles officially split up.
1971	September 3: John and Yoko Ono Lennon leave Great Britain for New York.
	October 8: The album *Imagine* is released.
1973	October: John and Yoko split up. John spends nearly eighteen months in his "lost weekend" period. He releases three albums: *Mind Games* in November 1973, *Walls and Bridges* in October 1974, and *Rock 'n' Roll* in February 1975.
1975	John and Yoko reunite and Yoko becomes pregnant.
	October 9: On John's thirty-fifth birthday, their son, Sean, is born.
1976	April: John Lennon retires from the music business and becomes a "house husband."
	July 27: John receives his green card, which grants him residency in the United States.
1980	August: John comes out of retirement and starts work in a recording studio again.
	November 17: The album *Double Fantasy* is released. It is John's first album for more than five years and is received with wide acclaim.
	December 8: John Lennon, at age forty, is murdered in New York by Mark Chapman.
	December 14: A ten-minute silence is observed worldwide in celebration of John Lennon's memory.

Recommended Listening

• **Singles with the Beatles:** "Please, Please Me," "Twist and Shout," "She Loves You," "Eleanor Rigby," "Strawberry Fields Forever," "Lucy in the Sky With Diamonds," All You Need Is Love."

• **Albums:** *Please, Please Me; A Hard Day's Night; Help!; Sgt. Pepper's Lonely Hearts Club Band.*

• **Singles as an independent artist:** "Give Peace a Chance," "Power to the People," "Happy Christmas (War Is Over)," "Mind Games," "Whatever Gets You Thru the Night," "Imagine," "Woman."

• **Albums as an independent artist:** *Imagine, Double Fantasy.*

Glossary

acoustic: Nonelectric.

bass guitar: A four-string electric guitar with steel strings.

blasphemy: A statement or action that disgraces God or sacred beliefs.

guru: A Hindu spiritual leader or head of a religious sect.

hallucinogenic: A type of drug that makes users believe they can see and hear people, animals, and objects that are not there.

jazz: A type of music with a strong rhythm that originated in the southern states in the early twentieth century.

Ku Klux Klan: A secret organization founded by southern whites to fight the effort to grant African Americans civil rights. It upheld its extreme religious views with violence, and lynched and murdered many civil rights activists. Although still active, it is less influential than it was in the 1960s.

LSD: Lysergic acid, a hallucinogenic drug.

diethylamide: A powerful hallucinogenic drug.

marijuana: The dried leaves, flowers, and stems of a plant, smoked or otherwise consumed as a drug.

phenomenon: A person or thing that is remarkable for an outstanding achievement or quality.

psychedelic: The expansion of the mind through the use of hallucinogenic drugs. The mind's awareness is supposedly increased with vivid sounds and unusual sights.

Royal Variety Show: A show that takes place every year in London in the presence of the monarch and members of the royal family.

sitar: An Indian musical instrument, a long-necked lute whose strings are plucked, giving an Eastern influence to music.

skiffle: A type of music that was popular in Great Britain in the 1950s. Its main characteristic was the use of improvised percussion instruments, such as bottles, washboards, and tea chests.

subversive: A person who tries to go against or overthrow authority.

Vietnam War: The war that took place after the division of Indochina in 1954 between Communist North Vietnam and South Vietnam. Initially, the United States supported South Vietnam with military aid, but sent troops in 1964 after two United States' destroyers were attacked by the North Vietnamese. Because of the unpopularity of the war in the United States, American troops were withdrawn in 1973. The war ended in 1975 when South Vietnam fell to the Communists.

Index